IMAGES
of Rail

SAN DIEGO
TROLLEYS

Enjoy the history!

[signature]

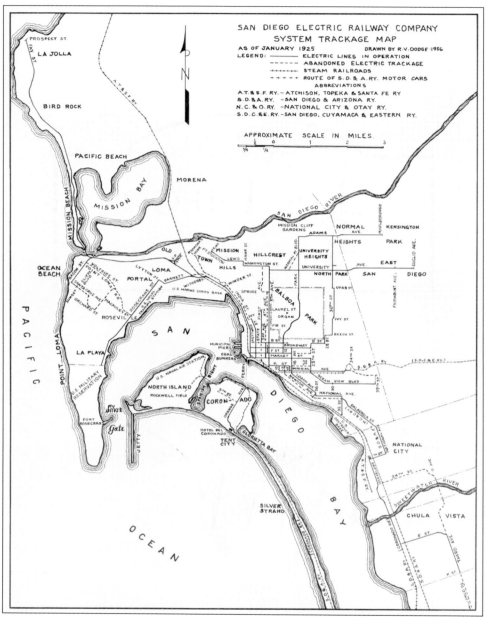

The San Diego Electric Railway (SDERy) was founded in 1891 by John D. Spreckels. The map here shows the SDERy at its maximum extent in 1925, stretching from La Jolla to the Mexican border. Also represented are bus (motor coach), ferry, and steam railroad lines owned or operated by Spreckels. (Courtesy of Richard V. Dodge.)

ON THE COVER: Passengers board San Diego & Southeastern Railroad (SD&SE) car No. 101 and trailer around 1915. Looking north on Third Avenue from Broadway, the U.S. Grant Hotel and Superba Theatre can be seen on the right. An offshoot of the National City & Otay Railroad, the SD&SE was an electric interurban line serving San Diego and National City. (Courtesy of the Pacific Southwest Railway Museum.)

IMAGES
of Rail

SAN DIEGO
TROLLEYS

Douglas W. Mengers

ARCADIA
PUBLISHING

Published by Arcadia Publishing
Charleston, South Carolina

Printed in the United States of America

Library of Congress Control Number: 2017946459

For all general information, please contact Arcadia Publishing:
Telephone 843-853-2070
Fax 843-853-0044
E-mail sales@arcadiapublishing.com
For customer service and orders:
Toll-Free 1-888-313-2665

Visit us on the Internet at www.arcadiapublishing.com

For Anna and our dreams.

CONTENTS

ACKNOWLEDGMENTS

This project is the result of many people working in the background to provide advice, direction, and resources. Dennis Gallegos provided the initial spark and has been an invaluable professional mentor. Mike Reading and Richard Finch generously provided access to the San Diego Electric Railway Association photograph archives and frequently directed me to valuable material I was unaware of. Bruce Semelsberger of the Pacific Southwest Railway Museum shared his extensive knowledge of the Southwest Railway Library collections and spent many hours locating and scanning photographs. Christine Travers, Carol Myers, and Natalie Fiocre of the San Diego History Center were a pleasure to work with as we dove deep into their photographic archives, ironing out kinks along the way. Likewise, Stephanie Washburn of the Coronado Historical Association was a great help in tracking down specific photographs taken in Coronado.

Michael Taylor and NWB Environmental Services LLC, a San Diego–based cultural resource management firm specializing in a comprehensive array of archaeological services, provided financial resources, without which this project would not have been possible. My employer, Alice Brewster, and PanGIS Inc., a consulting firm that specializes in archaeological, GIS, and environmental compliance, provided the financial support and scheduling flexibility to complete this project. Finally, Anna Graham Shonle of Graham Edits provided developmental editing and proofreading services for this project, the quality of which are known primarily to myself.

Thank you to all the above persons and organizations for helping to take this project from the idea stage to the final product. All your time and efforts are greatly appreciated.

Unless otherwise noted, the images in this volume appear courtesy of Aaron R. Duggan, PyroCat Photo/Graphic (AD); Alberto Foglia, MA, RPA (AF); the Coronado Historical Association (CHA); the author (DM); the Orange Empire Railway Museum (OERM); the Pacific Southwest Railway Museum (PSRM); the San Diego Electric Railway Association (SDERA); and the San Diego History Center (SDHC).

INTRODUCTION

San Diego's historical trolleys are receiving renewed interest lately with the centennial of the 1915–1916 Panama-California World Exposition. The expo marked the introduction of over 100 modern (for their time) Arts and Crafts–style trolley cars to a greatly expanding public transportation system. Over the last decade, historical streetcars from this era have been restored by museums and citizen groups, and plans are being discussed to reestablish the old trolley line serving Balboa Park museums and the San Diego Zoo. The expo period is only a small part of the story of San Diego's historical trolleys. The first horse-drawn streetcars of the 1880s, including those of the San Diego Streetcar Company, connected the commercial core of Alonzo Horton's new downtown to nearby wharves and resort hotels. A similar system operated on Coronado, connected to San Diego by a ferry across the bay.

A series of boom and bust cycles occurred in San Diego between the 1870s and 1890s. Some were magnified by local issues, such as rumors of a transcontinental railroad connection; others were the result of broader national economic forces. Regardless of the cause, they played out in San Diego as massive influxes and outflows of population, and the rise and collapse of businesses of every size, including those related to transportation. City development came in spurts with the booms and came to a halt with the busts. The arrival of electrification in the 1880s coincided with a growth in municipal services, including street lighting and water and sewer services.

Experiments with electrically powered streetcars soon began using this newly harnessed energy source to replace animal power for public transportation. While short-lived, the Electric Rapid Transit venture was an encouraging example of the wide-ranging uses of new technology being used to address urban problems. In the late 1890s, the San Diego Cable Railroad, a cable-driven streetcar system, like that successfully operated in San Francisco, was built. It too failed after a short time—a victim of the boom and bust cycle.

John D. Spreckels, a wealthy industrialist from San Francisco, began investing in San Diego infrastructure in the late 1880s. He oversaw construction of a commercial coaling wharf and bought into existing struggling ventures such as the Hotel Del Coronado, the San Diego and Coronado Ferry, and the Otay Water Company. In 1891, Spreckels formed the San Diego Electric Railway Company (SDERy). He began buying and consolidating several of San Diego's failed or failing transportation lines and began a process of massive expansion. By 1910, Spreckels's SDERy would be the only remaining trolley operator in San Diego. The stability provided by a large, centralized trolley network ushered in a new age of public transportation in San Diego. Spreckels's maxim that "transportation determines the flow of population" was perfectly timed to take advantage of a massive increase in population in San Diego and the greater Southern California region. This population movement, known as the Midwestern Migration, saw San Diego's population increase tenfold by the mid-1920s and politically, economically, and culturally transformed California from the periphery to the core.

The new SDERy routes extended into barren scrubland and paved the way for new neighborhoods that are in revival today, such as North Park, or are the core of historic districts, such as Mission Hills. New power plants, other facilities, and modern trolley cars were introduced over the next decade as planning for the 1915–1916 expo ramped up. The trolley lines served to bring commuters to the downtown area for work and shopping. They also provided transportation to new destinations built by the trolley companies and other developers, including picnic grounds, public baths, and amusement parks.

After the exposition, however, the system began to decline; the costs of materials increased during World War I, and funding was diverted by Spreckels to a railroad connection to the east. Even so, a major upgrade and repair project took place in the 1920s, along with the introduction of many modern cars. Once a new rapid line to the beach communities to the north was opened mid-decade, SDERy achieved its maximum extent.

Meanwhile, autobuses were also introduced in the 1920s on some temporary or low-traffic routes, and private automobiles were being used more often. Although a successful new streetcar was introduced in the 1930s and traffic picked up during the 1935–1936 expo, electric trolleys waned in use through the 1930s, not only in San Diego but across the country. After a brief resurgence during World War II, during which many obsolete streetcars from across the United States were temporarily added, the entire system was converted to autobuses by 1949. After the war, most of the old wooden cars were sold for scrap or destroyed. Some were sold to private individuals and converted to housing or commercial use. A group of the more modern cars were transferred to another streetcar network and saw more years of service. Wires were removed, and track was paved over or pulled up and recycled. Facilities were adapted for buses, sold to the local electrical utility, or demolished. Within a few short years, little trace of San Diego's electric streetcars remained.

For the next three decades, public transportation in San Diego consisted entirely of buses and the Coronado Ferry. However, in 1981, a new light rail system debuted. It proved successful and has continued to serve San Diego into the 21st century, with regular expansions and a fleet of modern cars. The current San Diego Trolley serves more riders and an area much larger than SDERy did at its maximum extent. A Mid-Coast Trolley extension to La Jolla is currently under construction. San Diego's Regional Transportation Plan for 2050 includes the possibility of extending the system to cover many areas not served since SDERy shut down, including Balboa Park, Pacific Beach, and Hillcrest, as well as a line to the airport.

The old trolleys were gone but not forgotten. The last decade has seen a developing nostalgia for the early electric streetcars, partially driven by the centennial of the 1915–1916 expo. Communities on the old streetcar lines incorporate the historical trolleys in their identity, museums and citizen groups have restored trolley cars, and the Metropolitan Transit System has added restored cars to service on the Silver Line downtown.

The remains of the SDERy and earlier streetcar systems are being uncovered during construction projects across San Diego. Combined with historical documents, the material remains can tell us the untold stories of San Diegans from the 1880s to the 1940s. How San Diegans of the past interacted with public transportation is relevant today. Today's trolley system has been serving San Diego for approximately half of the time that SDERy was in business. Lessons can be learned from the past.

One

HORSE-DRAWN
STREETCARS

A horse-drawn streetcar carries passengers along Fifth Street in this c. 1886 photograph. A single set of tracks running down the center of the street connected San Diego's wharf area to the commercial core. Electricity had arrived in San Diego several years earlier, as evidenced by wired poles along the sidewalks and the arc light just right of center in the background. (SDHC.)

Elisha Babcock, pictured here in 1900, was already a successful businessman when he arrived in San Diego in the 1880s. Having liquidated his assets in his home state of Indiana, he and a small group of investors bought the Coronado peninsula in 1885. The following year, they established a string of businesses aimed at developing the area between San Diego Bay and the Pacific Ocean. (SDHC.)

One of Babcock's first projects in the area was establishing the San Diego and Coronado Ferry Company with fellow investor Hampton L. Story. As part of the project, they had a ferry landing built on the bay side of the peninsula to receive future residents and tourists. The 100-foot wooden-hulled side-paddle steamer *Coronado*, pictured here, made its first run on April 16, 1886. (CHA.)

Later that year, the Coronado Beach Company was formed to develop the southern half of the peninsula, including design of a street grid, grading and landscaping of lots, and installation of water supply and irrigation systems. This photograph shows lots being auctioned, which began on November 13, 1886. Investors recouped the entire purchase price of the peninsula, with 350 lots sold on the first day of the auction. (CHA.)

The jewel in the crown of Babcock and Story's Coronado development was the Hotel Del Coronado. The ground-breaking ceremony for the luxury seaside resort, the finest in the West, occurred on March 19, 1887. When the hotel opened on February 19, 1888, "the Del" was the largest resort hotel in the world. (SDHC.)

Babcock and Story organized the first public transit company in San Diego, the San Diego Streetcar Company, in 1886. The ferry landing was connected by rail to the Hotel Del Coronado. Horse-drawn cars, built by the Pullman Company and St. Louis Car Company, seated 16 to 32 passengers depending on configuration. Service began July 3, 1886. Pictured here is one of the original cars, restored by a private collector. (SDERA.)

The San Diego Streetcar Company served both Coronado and the downtown San Diego area. To meet the needs of both segments, streetcar barns were built with room for 15 to 20 cars and 100 horses each, as well as hay lofts, blacksmith shops, and corrals. Seen here is the Coronado car barn near the ferry landing in 1887. (CHA.)

Horton chose to build his family residence on the mesa top about halfway between Old Town and the new downtown area. The area was just west of a large tract of undeveloped land set aside as City Park, which would later become Balboa Park. Horton and his wife, Sarah, are seen here in front of the Horton residence at First and Fir Streets in 1887. (SDHC.)

The neighborhood north of downtown was named Florence Heights after the new Florence Hotel. Here, a horsecar appears on Fir Street between Third and Fourth Streets in 1888 just before the opening of the streetcar line to the hotel. On the flat downtown area, streetcars were pulled by a team of two horses, and a third horse was added for runs up the hill to the hotel and beyond. (SDHC.)

William Wallace Bowers, Alonzo Horton's brother-in-law, arrived in San Diego in 1869. Bowers, a successful hotelier, was hired by Horton to build Horton House in 1870. Bowers managed Horton House until 1873, after which he served in the California State Assembly and as customs collector for the port of San Diego. In 1883, Bowers built his own hotel, the Florence Hotel, which would cater to the tourist trade. (SDHC.)

Built on the mesa north of downtown and commanding excellent views from its widow's walk, the Florence Hotel promoted San Diego's excellent climate for health and relaxation. The hotel was not named after the Italian city, but instead, Bowers intended the name to be a reference to flowers. The Florence Hotel can be seen here shortly after its opening in January 1884. (SDHC.)

Within the first year after opening, the hotel's veranda was enclosed with glass, providing a conservatory for the guests, seen here in 1884. Horse-drawn carriages were provided between downtown and the train station. The San Diego Streetcar Line originally ran up Fourth Street adjacent to the hotel. Also during the hotel's first year, a spur line was added on Fir Street directly in front of the hotel. (SDHC.)

The Florence Hotel originally offered 43 guest rooms and was an instant success; winter bookings filled up almost immediately. Many of the rooms had fireplaces, and every room had windows allowing guests to take advantage of the view. The hotel quickly became a social center for wealthier tourists. The rotunda, seen here around 1887, was outfitted with the finest furnishings and décor available. (SDHC.)

In addition to the informal parlor for socializing, pictured here in 1887, guests could take advantage of both public and private dining rooms, a dance floor on the veranda, and separate billiard rooms for men and women. All of the modern conveniences were on hand: an annunciator system for room service, soundproofed rooms, and a telephone. (SDHC.)

Within the hotel's first year, construction began on an additional wing and guest cottages across the street. Bowers sold the hotel after returning to politics in 1890 when he was elected San Diego's first congressman. The new owner and manager, John C. Fisher, was general manager of San Diego's next public transit system, the San Diego Cable Railway. Seen here in 1891, the Florence Hotel eventually offered 275 rooms. (SDHC.)

Two

EARLY ELECTRIC AND CABLE CARS

After the success of San Francisco's cable cars in 1873, many other cities installed similar systems. The San Diego Cable Car Company was the fourth system in California, following Oakland and Los Angeles, and lasted just over a year. Here, a cable car travels southbound on Sixth Street near Market Street about 1891. (SDHC.)

San Diego's cable cars ran on portions of a track system laid for a short-lived electric trolley line called Electric Rapid Transit Company (ERT). ERT was headed by George Copeland, a local businessman who was also the president of the San Diego Flume Company, established in 1886 to bring water from the Cuyamaca Mountains to San Diego. Pictured here is the flume's Los Coches Trestle near Flinn Springs in 1898. (SDHC.)

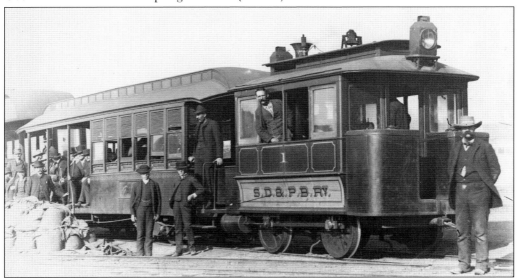

Copeland secured an arrangement with the San Diego & Old Town Street Railway to test an electric trolley system on a section of its steam locomotive line, seen here about 1890. Copeland had an electrical generating plant built and had poles and wire installed along Kettner (formerly Atlantic) Street between downtown and Old Town. On November 19, 1887, he successfully ran the first electric trolley in the West along this route. (PSRM.)

The following month, Copeland organized the Electric Rapid Transit Company. The poles and wires along Kettner Street were moved several blocks east to Fourth Street. The southern terminus of the line was the Pacific Coast Steamship wharf. Pictured here is one of the ERT cars on the wharf about 1888. (SDERA.)

From the wharf area, the ERT line ran north through the center of downtown. Cars were open-style with bench seating. Operators of the trolleys were referred to as "motioneers." Seen here is an ERT car in front of a Victorian house on Fourth Street north of downtown in 1889. (SDHC.)

From downtown, the line continued up Fourth Street to Fir Street and the Florence Hotel, seen here in 1888. Service began on December 31, 1887. The route was deemed an early success and plans were immediately made to extend the line farther north. The areas surrounding downtown had seen increasing residential development during the boom years of the 1880s. (SDHC.)

The ERT laid additional rail, extending the line north to the new neighborhood of University Heights. University Heights was established by the College Hill Land Association in 1887, and by 1888, streets were being graded, water and sewer service was established, and lots were offered for sale. An ERT trolley can be seen here pulling several unpowered trailer cars on upper Fourth Street about 1888. (SDERA.)

One 24,600-foot cable powered the "town" section at eight miles per hour. This line ran from a turntable on L Street near the Pacific Coast Steamship wharf, north on Sixth Street, west on C Street, and north on Fourth Street past the Florence Hotel to the power station. The cable sat in a channel below street level restrained by iron yokes every five feet, as illustrated here. (PSRM.)

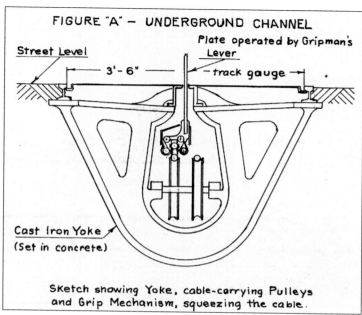

FIGURE "A" – UNDERGROUND CHANNEL

Street Level

Plate operated by Gripman's Lever

3'-6"

track gauge

Cast Iron Yoke (Set in concrete)

Sketch showing Yoke, cable-carrying Pulleys and Grip Mechanism, squeezing the cable.

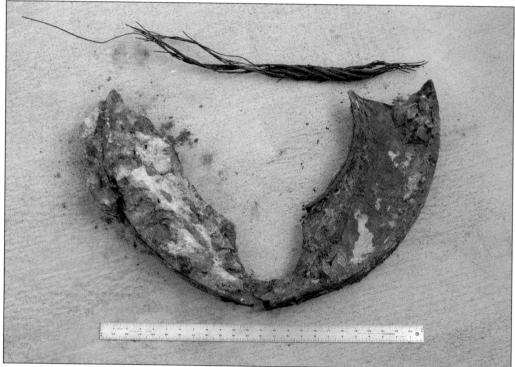

Another 27,000-foot cable powered the "mesa" section, the high-speed portion running 10 miles per hour. This route ran north along Fourth Street, east on University Avenue, north on Normal Street and Park Boulevard to another turntable at Adams Avenue. Seen here is a portion of cable and yoke recovered during archaeological excavations just south of the powerhouse location in 2003. (AD.)

Two hundred men worked for two months trenching for the town section's underground cable, completed on October 2, 1889. Pictured is a San Diego Pioneer Truck Company horse team hauling the cable spools for installation. Most cable car lines feature two sets of tracks: one outbound and one inbound. San Diego's, however, primarily ran on a single set of tracks that used strategic turnouts for the passing of cars. (SDHC.)

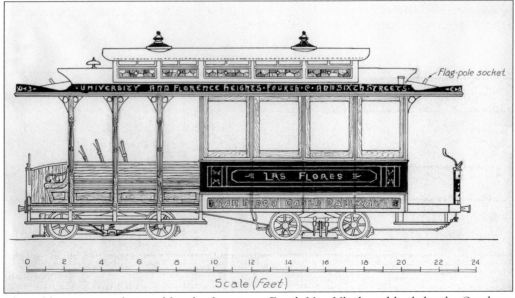

The cable cars were designed by chief engineer Frank Van Vleck and built by the Stockton Combine, Harvester & Agricultural Works of Stockton, California. The cars had stained-glass clerestory windows, battery-powered push-button electric bells for signaling stops, and two sets of wheels per truck for smooth operation. This is a design sketch of a typical car. (SDHC.)

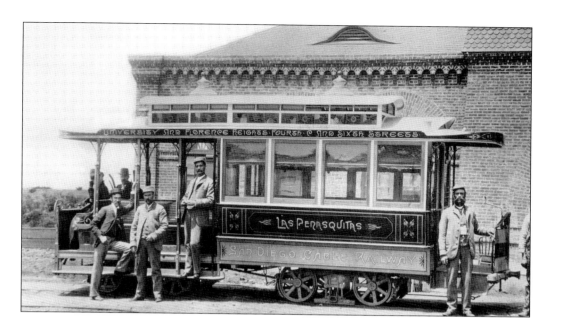

The cars had a maroon and gray paint scheme, white roofs, and gold lettering. Unlike most cars, those of the San Diego Cable Railway were not numbered. Instead, they were given local names including *Cuyamaca*, *El Cajon*, and *La Jolla*. Twelve cars were built, most featuring a combination style with one open end and the other end enclosed with glass windows. Seen above is the *Las Penasquitas* car and crew at the cable car power station in 1890 or 1891. Designer Van Vleck can be seen at far left with his foot on the running board. Below is the *San Ysidora* car on the turntable in front of the power station in 1891. (Both, SDHC.)

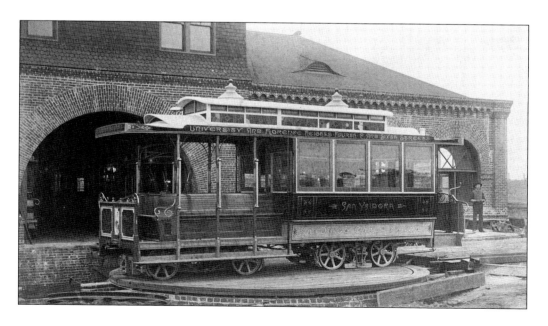

The car operator, or gripman, used a lever to grip the continuously moving cable to pull the car along. Gripmen, who enjoyed a fairly prestigious job for the time, were paid 18¢ an hour. Seen here in front of the power station in 1890, the gripmen provided their own uniforms and caps of grey wool, bearing insignia color based on rank. (SDHC.)

The San Diego Cable Railway constructed a boarding house adjacent to the power station for bachelor gripmen. Crew and cars can be seen here at the power station in 1890 shortly before opening day. The car in the power station entry was one of two additional trailer cars that could be towed behind grip cars when extra passenger space was needed. (SDHC.)

Opening day on June 7, 1890, began with a downtown parade of seven of the new cable cars. The City Guard Band boarded the *El Escondido* car, seen here on Sixth Street, which was decked out for the occasion in red, white, and blue bunting. In the background is the *San Juan Capistrano* car. (SDHC.)

The parade stopped at the Brewster Hotel downtown, seen here in 1891, where important figures including Mayor Douglas Gunn and California governor Robert Waterman hopped on. Local horticulturist Kate Sessions was the first paying customer. The parade continued to the powerhouse for speeches and a tour of the machinery. The Brewster Hotel would later play a grim role in the collapse of the San Diego Cable Railway. (SDHC.)

Traveling toward the mesa summit, the cable car route passed the Florence Hotel at Fourth and Fir Streets. San Diego Cable Railway vice president John C. Fisher became owner and operator of the hotel in 1890. As enhancements to the property, Fisher planted Moreton Bay fig trees, seen here in 1891 behind the cable car. One of the trees, San Diego Historic Landmark No. 53, still exists on the north side of the property. The hotel itself eventually became apartments and then a retirement home. It was demolished in the 1940s. The neighborhood north of Florence Heights, soon to be known as Hillcrest, was just beginning to be developed in the 1890s. The San Diego Cable Railway constructed a recreational park on University Avenue near Tenth Street in 1890. The park had grandstands, and baseball games, bicycle races, and other sporting events were held there. (SDHC.)

In the late 19th and early 20th century, public transit companies often built amusement parks or other attractions at the ends of routes to boost ridership. The San Diego Cable Railway was no exception. The University Heights area was still sparsely settled at the time, and the railway established a music pavilion and public park at "the Bluffs" at the northern terminus of the line, pictured here in 1890. (SDHC.)

The Pavilion at the Bluffs provided indoor spaces for concerts and dancing, and was surrounded by five acres of picnic and strolling grounds. Orchestra concerts were held every Sunday, and a merry-go-round and shooting gallery were later added. Pictured is the Pavilion at the Bluffs shortly after opening on September 9, 1890. (SDHC.)

The pavilion, pictured here, sat atop the bluffs above Mission Valley, which at the time was dairy farm territory. The pavilion and landscaped terraces provided an excellent view of the Pacific Ocean to the west. The San Diego Cable Railway planned to extend the line down into the valley to Mission San Diego de Alcala. The railway was successful, although construction and operating costs were much higher than expected. (SDHC.)

Here, the walking trails below the Pavilion at the Bluffs can be seen. The San Diego Cable Railway project was doomed by the abrupt collapse of the California National Bank, the railway's backer, in November 1891. An investigation revealed mismanagement by the bank, including risky loans and embezzlement, and showed that the San Diego Cable Railway had not received all of the funds it was due. (SDHC.)

Bank president David Dare was in Europe at the time of the crash and simply never returned. Treasurer J.W. Collins committed suicide in the Brewster Hotel. It eventually came to light that Dare and Collins had embezzled $800,000 from the bank. The railway struggled along with reduced and interrupted service until October 15, 1892, when a judge ordered that it be shut down. Although new cable was sitting at the dock where it had arrived, the railway lacked the funds to install it. Eventually, the surplus cable was sold to Madame Tingley of the Theosophical Institute in Point Loma where it was used for fencing the extensive compound. The institute was a utopian community associated with spiritualist Madame Blavatsky. It included an elaborate temple, a community theater, self-sustaining agricultural land, and a Raja Yoga boarding school for children. The Theosophical Institute and its surrounding cable fence are seen here about 1900. (SDHC.)

In August 1895, George Kerper of Cincinnati bought the remnants of the San Diego Cable Railway for $17,600. He organized the Citizens Traction Company and came to San Diego to convert the cable railway to electric service. Citizens Traction replaced the cable winders in the powerhouse with electric generators and installed poles and overhead wiring along the same route used by the cable cars. Nine cable cars were converted to electric service, seen here at the entrance to the recreation park at Tenth Street and University Avenue in 1896. On July 28, 1896, service on the line began, with five cars in regular service. The Pavilion at the Bluffs was restored and its name changed to Mission Cliff Gardens. Citizens Traction eventually planned to build an inclined railway down the bluffs into Mission Valley and out to the Mission San Diego de Alcala. Unfortunately, financial problems related to high operating costs began within a few months. Citizens Traction was unable to meet payroll and other debts and was closed down and put up for auction in February 1898. (PSRM.)

Three

SAN DIEGO ELECTRIC RAILWAY AND CONSOLIDATION

Several electric trolleys can be seen here at the intersection of Fifth and Market Streets in 1893. Hung on the single-deck car in the foreground is a banner advertising a pageant at the Fisher Opera House, owned by John C. Fisher of the San Diego Cable Railway and Florence Hotel. Built in 1892, the Fisher was the finest theater on the West Coast. (PSRM.)

John D. Spreckels, pictured at left in the 1890s, was deeply involved in the development of San Diego in the late 19th and early 20th centuries. His first visit to San Diego occurred in 1887 at the height of the boom when he sailed his yacht *Lurline*, seen below about 1910, into San Diego Bay to reprovision. Spreckels's father, Claus Spreckels, was an industrialist with a vast sugar empire in Hawaii and the San Francisco Bay area. In the early 1880s, John Spreckels had established a successful shipping line serving both of these ports as well as Australia, New Zealand, and several Pacific islands. When Spreckels arrived in San Diego, his money and business reputation attracted the attention of the town council, which immediately offered him a franchise to build a coaling wharf. Spreckels accepted, envisioning San Diego as the finest city on the West Coast. (Both, SDHC.)

During his first visit to San Diego, Spreckels met Elisha Babcock, whose Hotel Del, seen here in 1887, was under construction. Babcock was having financial difficulties due to exorbitant construction costs and was seeking additional investors. Spreckels bought into the Coronado Beach Company and, within a year, had bought out the shares of investor Hampton Story. (SDHC.)

By 1889, Spreckels and his brother Adolph purchased the remainder of the Coronado Beach Company, becoming sole owners of the real estate development, the Hotel Del Coronado, the Coronado Beach Railroad, and the Coronado Ferry. Included with the hotel were the boathouse and bathhouse, pictured here in 1897, as well as ice manufacturing and electricity distribution. In 1892, Spreckels also acquired the San Diego Streetcar Company. (CHA.)

On the San Diego side of the bay, Spreckels and his brother Adolph formed the Spreckels Brothers Commercial Company and constructed an elaborate coaling wharf, seen here around 1897. Rail was laid on the long wharf, and a system of bunkers and hoists was installed to enable direct unloading of coal from ship holds to train cars, a great improvement over the former method using small tender boats. (SDHC.)

Spreckels believed that for his investments to return a favorable profit, San Diego would need to grow. And for San Diego to grow, a consistent water source was essential. Spreckels invested in Babcock's Otay Water Company, which built four dams in the San Diego backcountry, connected to the city by wooden flumes and pipelines. Seen here is the Dulzura Conduit near Barrett Junction in 1915. (SDHC.)

In addition to water, Spreckels believed that reliable transportation connecting new residential areas to downtown was essential. To that end, he began to consolidate and expand the various transportation ventures he controlled. This started with the incorporation of the San Diego Electric Railway Company (SDERy) on November 30, 1891. The new company logo is seen here (SDERA.)

As incorporated, the board of directors for the SDERy included John D. Spreckels as director, his brother Adolph, seen here around 1920, as president, and Elisha Babcock as vice president. William Clayton, general manager, would eventually become vice president and managing director of all Spreckels companies. Incorporation of SDERy included a provision for acquiring the San Diego Streetcar Company, which suffered a decline in business after the boom. (SDHC.)

Creditors filed claims against the San Diego Streetcar Company in 1889. It was acquired by SDERy in January 1892 for $115,000. This included eight-and-a-half miles of track, 30 horse cars, the corrals and car barns in San Diego and Coronado, and nearly 150 horses and their tack and other equipment. Here, a horsecar is seen at the corner of Fifth and E Streets in the late 1880s. (PSRM.)

The transfer of the Coronado Beach Company to Spreckels also included two steam railroad lines that had failed with the end of the boom. One of these was the Park Belt (or University Heights) Motor Road. Built by Babcock and Story, it began service on July 7, 1888. It was designed to serve new residential communities in the Choate addition, whose real estate offices are seen here in 1885. (SDHC.)

The Motor Road began at Eighteenth and A Streets in Golden Hill where San Diego Streetcar service ended. Seen here in a 1956 illustration, cars were disconnected from the horse teams and connected to a small steam engine that ran east and north through Switzer Canyon, past an isolation camp that had been built to house victims of a smallpox outbreak in 1887. (PSRM.)

The Motor Road, pictured decades after abandonment, continued up the canyons toward empty land near University and Marlborough Avenues. It then looped west along University Avenue, Florida Canyon, and Essex Street and turned south down Fifth Street to reconnect with the horsecar system near the Florence Hotel. The line failed by October 1889 with the collapse of the boom. SDERy later acquired the trackage and right-of-way. (PSRM.)

The Coronado Railroad, founded in 1886, was another Babcock and Story project that failed at the end of the boom. Steam trains, seen here in 1886, originally ran from the ferry landing to the Hotel Del Coronado. The rail was extended down the Silver Strand the following year in time for the auction of lots at Coronado Heights (which was later part of Imperial Beach). (CHA.)

In 1888, the line was extended around the south end of San Diego Bay and up to downtown San Diego, as shown in this 1910 realty brochure. Competition from the National City and Otay Railroad and declining ridership from the bust led to financial difficulties. The Coronado Railroad was included as part of the Coronado Beach Company sale to Spreckels in December 1891. (SDHC.)

With the acquisition of the horsecar and steam lines, SDERy began the process of converting the entire system to run on electricity in early 1892. This included relaying of the track to a common gauge and adding passing tracks throughout the downtown area. Horse-drawn work cars, like the tower car from the 1890s shown here, were used to install and repair overhead wires. (SDERA.)

A power plant was built in 1892 at Kettner Street and Broadway. Its 125-foot smokestack is visible in this 1900 image. Inside, a 300-horsepower steam engine drove two 100-kilowatt generators. Additional machinery was added in 1893 and 1896 as demand increased. The plant building was sold to San Diego Gas & Electric in 1921, and today, the façade remains as part of the Electra condominium tower. (SDHC.)

Ten new electric trolley cars were bought from the J.G. Brill Company of Philadelphia in 1892. Cars Nos. 1 and 2, shown here, were the first double-decker cars in the West. The lower center sections were enclosed with three windows on each side, and the ends were open. Extension platforms accommodated stairs on each end to reach the upper deck. Seating accommodated 48 passengers. (SDERA.)

Passenger service was inaugurated on September 21, 1892, with a VIP run pictured here at the corner of Fifth and Market Streets that included Alonzo Horton, John Fisher, Elisha Babcock, and other civic notables. By the end of the year, SDERy comprised 12.2 miles of electric track and 4.5 miles of horse-car service. (SDHC.)

The cars were painted yellow, with gold leaf and brown stenciling. Car No. 1 is seen here in front of Marston's department store at Fifth and C Streets in about 1896. Store owner George Marston arrived in San Diego in 1870 as a teenager and, by the time of this photograph, had served on the city council and the first public library board. (SDERA.)

Unlike earlier cable cars, the electric trolleys could operate in reverse, eliminating the need for turntables at the end of each line. Car No. 2 is seen here around 1895 serving the Fifth Street and Logan Heights Line, one of the earliest lines to be electrified. Replacing horse-car service, it ran from University Avenue through downtown to new residential and industrial areas southeast of downtown. (SDERA.)

Cars Nos. 3 through 8 were single-deck trolleys, otherwise similar in design to the double-deckers, with a closed center section and open ends and seating for 22 passengers. One of these cars can be seen here around 1892, in a view looking south on Fifth Street from E Street. Replacing existing horse-car service, the Depot Line terminated at the Pacific Coast Steamship wharf and nearby National City & Otay (NC&O) and Coronado Railroad depots at the foot of Fifth Street. On the left is the Baroque façade of the Bank of Commerce, which later housed the Louis Oyster Bar, a favorite of Wyatt Earp's, and the Golden Poppy Hotel, a brothel run by Madam Cora. Arc lamps, like those seen on the right, were mounted on 100-foot masts around the commercial district downtown. Public reaction to the lamps, which were invented by Charles Brush of Cleveland in 1879, was mixed. Although they lit a much wider area than gas lamps, the light was cold and harsh compared to the soft yellow glow of gas. (SDHC.)

The other end of the Depot Line terminated at the California Southern Railroad depot built in 1887 at the foot of Broadway. The California Southern, completed in 1885, ran from National City to Barstow, California. It connected to the transcontinental Southern Pacific Railroad at Colton, providing service to and from Chicago. Here, one of the Nos. 3 through 8 series trolleys can be seen at the depot around 1899. (PSRM.)

The Coronado Ferry was slipped at the Santa Fe Railroad wharf at the foot of Market Street. The SDERy Ferry Line ran downtown from the wharf, up to the Southern California Railway depot, across to Fifth Street, and back down to Market Street. Here, one of the Nos. 3 through 8 series trolleys is seen on the wharf around 1895. (SDHC.)

Cars Nos. 9 and 10 were semi-closed type, originally with canvas roll-up shades installed in six openings along each side of the body. Later, windows replaced the shades, as pictured here on Fifth Street in the 1890s. In 1895, a former horsecar was converted to a similar windowed car and numbered 11. These were popularly referred to as boxcars. (SDHC.)

In 1893, four horsecar bodies were converted to electric service by adding motors and trolley poles. Numbered 12 through 15, they were open body style, seating 32 passengers. Car No. 15 is seen here in 1902 on Market Street heading toward Fifth Street. In the horse-drawn buckboard is William Frederick "Buffalo Bill" Cody, in a parade to promote his Wild West exhibition later that day. (PSRM.)

D Street (today's Broadway) was electrified in 1893, from the car house near the California Southern Railroad depot to Eighteenth Street, replacing horsecar service. In 1895, the track was extended to Twenty-Fifth Street to serve the growing Golden Hill neighborhood. Seen here is one of the Nos. 3 through 8 series trolleys at D Street and Twenty-First Street about 1903. In 1896, First Street was electrified up to Laurel Street, with the first electric trolley service on June 30 replacing horse-car service on that route. These two routes were combined to form the First and D Streets Line shortly after. By the end of 1897, all 16.7 miles of track in the SDERy system had been electrified. Regarding his financing of the SDERy consolidation and buildup, Spreckels said, "I made those larger investments to protect the investments I had already made. It was just plain business sense." (SDHC.)

Popular destinations along the downtown trolley routes included San Diego's bathhouses. In the 1880s, this included the Caroline Bath House at the foot of Sixth Street, and W.W. Collier's, with special accommodations for women, at the foot of Fifth Street. These early bathhouses consisted of wooden tubs or pens built in the bay with slides, diving platforms, and swimming instructors. In the 1890s, more elaborate facilities were constructed, including the Tropical Natatorium at the foot of Broadway, which included electric lighting, steam baths, and an enormous indoor seawater pool. The most luxurious of the bathhouses was Los Baños, built by Graham Babcock (Elisha's son) in 1897 across from the California Southern Railroad depot on Broadway. Designed by architects William Hebbard and Irving Gill, the facility used steam from the adjacent SDERy power plant to heat the indoor saltwater pool. Amenities included locker rooms and showers, as well as slides, springboards, and hanging rings. The power plant smokestack can be seen behind Los Baños in the c. 1900 photographs above and below. (Both, SDHC.)

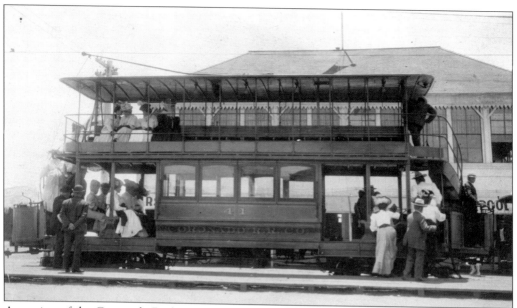

A portion of the Coronado Railroad was converted to electric service at about the same time as the SDERy. Two Brill trolley cars were purchased in 1893. Car No. 41, seen here, was a double-deck car like SDERy cars Nos. 1 and 2, but was longer. It carried 72 passengers and was primarily used for busier weekend service. Car No. 42 was single-deck, similar to SDERy cars Nos. 3 through 8. (CHA.)

The electrified route opened in October 1893 and ran along Orange Avenue from the ferry landing to the Hotel Del Coronado. Here, car No. 41 stands at the ferry landing in 1893. The various Spreckels transportation companies, including the SDERy, the San Diego and Coronado Ferry, and the Coronado Beach Railroad, operated together to provide regular service from Fifth Street and Broadway in downtown San Diego to the Hotel Del. (CHA.)

In early 1900, Spreckels levelled and expanded the sand spit south of the Hotel Del Coronado for construction of a waterfront entertainment complex known as Tent City, seen here in 1904. Several hundred furnished grass huts and canvas tents, some with electricity, were set up for weekly rental, with many hundreds more added over the next few years. More permanent structures housed a restaurant, a soda fountain, a grocery store, a library, and even a small hotel. The resort had its own newspaper, the *Daily Program*, which contained guest lists, concert schedules, and excursions available. Prior to 1906, visitors could walk from the SDERy terminal at the Hotel Del Coronado, or come around the south end of San Diego Bay up the Strand via Coronado Beach Railroad steam engine. Spreckels was originally unsure that Tent City would be popular enough to sustain itself and was concerned that it would siphon business away from the Hotel Del, but both worries turned out to be unfounded. (SDHC.)

Amenities also included a wading pool and merry-go-round, seen here. Picnic tables, a bandstand with free concerts, and a shooting gallery were also available to resort-goers. Animal attractions included a seal tank, an ostrich farm, monkeys, and a trick-performing horse. The resort was open from May to October each year, with Fourth of July being an exceptionally popular time to visit. (CHA.)

When the ferry boat *Silver Gate* was retired in 1903, it was set up on the bay side of Tent City as a floating dance pavilion and casino, as seen in this 1905 photograph. Eventually, a more permanent pavilion was constructed that contained a theater and bowling alley, along with a larger dance pavilion and casino. (CHA.)

SDERy acquired the assets of the failed Citizens Traction Company at auction in February 1898. The route from Mission Cliff Gardens to the intersection of Fifth Street and University Avenue was converted to SDERy's standard gauge rail, connected to its Fifth Street electric line, and service continued. The Mission Cliff Pavilion was reopened, as seen here on the banner of car No. 1, advertising a concert around 1900. (PSRM.)

About 1900, a trolley car body shop and a paint shop were constructed adjacent to the powerhouse at Kettner Street and Broadway. There in 1904, SDERy cars Nos. 1 and 2 were remodeled, and their upper decks removed. Car No. 1 is seen here after conversion in an undated photograph at the car maintenance shop at Fifteenth Street and Imperial Avenue. (SDERA.)

The removal of the upper decks of cars Nos. 1 and 2 was part of a complete car remodeling program for SDERy. With electric railways becoming popular throughout the United States, Europe, and South America, trolley car technology was advancing rapidly and cars from the early 1890s were already outdated. A new car built by American Car Company of St. Louis, Missouri, was delivered to SDERy in early 1902, numbered car 50. It was similar in design to Brill cars Nos. 3 through 8 but was longer, seating 36. This type of combination car, with a glass-enclosed center section and open ends with longitudinal seating, became known as "California cars." They were very popular with riders and came with the latest technological innovations, including advanced braking systems and electric motors. Car No. 50 can be seen in this c. 1904 view on Fifth Street, looking north from E Street. (SDHC.)

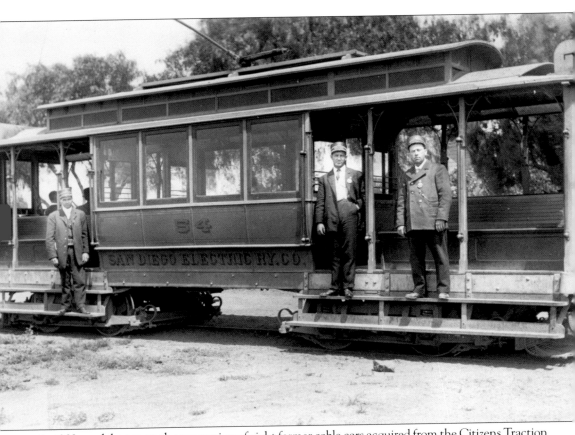

In 1902, work began on the conversion of eight former cable cars acquired from the Citizens Traction Company into four new extended-length California cars. Each car's end was removed, and it was joined to another to form a 33-foot-long closed-center car that seated 36. The clerestory windows of the earlier San Diego Cable Railroad design were retained. The car bodies were mounted on double trucks, resulting in much smoother operation. The four resulting cars were numbered 51 through 54 and were put in service in 1903. Seen here is car No. 54 shortly after introduction in 1903. This particular car was restored in the 1960s (see page 119). After stints at the Whaley House in Old Town and the San Diego History Center in Balboa Park, car No. 54 can now be viewed at the San Diego Electric Railway Association Museum in National City. (SDERA.)

Four

EXPANSION AND EXPOSITION

Here, several of the transportation options available in downtown San Diego in 1912 are visible looking north on Fifth Street at Market Street. SDERy cars Nos. 97 and 135 vie for space with automobiles, bicyclists, and horses. The mass of overhead wires shows the growth of both San Diego and the electric trolley system. (SDHC.)

Although their interests in San Diego were growing, the Spreckels family businesses were headquartered in San Francisco. After the great earthquake of 1906, however, John D. Spreckels permanently relocated to San Diego. He constructed a mansion on Glorietta Bay across from the Hotel Del Coronado, seen here in 1910, where he lived for the rest of his life. (CHA.)

A direct rail connection to the East had still not materialized for San Diego. Spreckels threw his weight into this venture by incorporating the San Diego & Arizona (SD&A) Railway on December 14, 1906, acquiring resources from a stalled plan by Marston and other San Diego businessmen. John Spreckels is seen in this 1910s photograph in front of one of the SD&A passenger cars. (CHA.)

A large expansion of the SDERy system began in 1904 with the introduction of new California-style cars, based on the successful design of the remodeled cable cars. Thirty of these were produced by 1908, numbered 57 through 86. Car No. 59 can be seen here at Fifth Street and Broadway in 1905. A new Imperial Avenue Line replaced the Depot Line in 1905, and was extended east to Mount Hope Cemetery in 1909. (SDHC.)

The new California cars had glass-enclosed center sections, open ends, and sat 36 passengers. Car No. 61 can be seen here in 1911 on the ferry wharf at the end of the new Market Street Line begun in 1907. The cars also saw service on the new Third Street Line that ran to the Florence Hotel by 1906 and was then extended to Mission Hills in 1907. (SDHC.)

Opening day festivities for the new Adams Avenue Line in 1907 are seen here, with cars Nos. 69 through 72 near Fortieth Street. The bridge over Texas Street was built in 1907. Once the bridge over Ward Canyon was built in 1910, the line was extended to what is today the Kensington neighborhood. Spreckels believed that if he built transit lines across the undeveloped mesas north and east of downtown, residential development would follow. He would recoup his investment

with each nickel fare. Unlike earlier boom and bust cycles, suburban San Diego settlement at the turn of the 20th century consisted not of speculators, but of families looking to build their own homes. A great number of these families came from the Midwest, drawn by advertising campaigns promoting the beautiful weather and cheap land of Southern California. (SDHC.)

The new University Avenue–City Heights Line opened in 1907, along the newly graded University Avenue. Just east of Park Boulevard, a redwood bridge, pictured here in 1907, was constructed to allow Georgia Street to cross the newly cut road and the SDERy tracks. A second set of tracks was laid along University Avenue in 1914. (PSRM.)

Like the Adams Avenue Line, the City Heights Line was built across the undeveloped mesas. Prior to grading and laying of track, only citrus and nut groves existed this far from the city center. Here, a service car and crew lay track along University Avenue near Florida Canyon in 1907. (PSRM.)

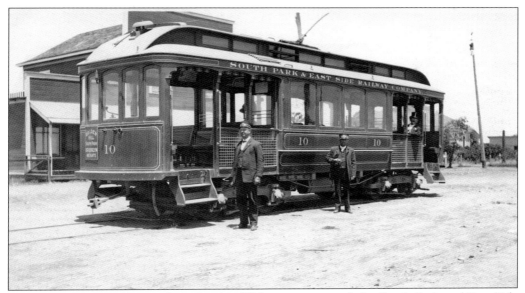

South and east of Balboa Park, E. Bartlett Webster constructed the South Park and East Side Railroad (SP&ES) to serve his new South Park residential development. Inaugurated in March 1906, the SP&ES initially ran from Twenty-Fifth Street and Broadway to Thirtieth and Cedar Streets, where a powerhouse was built. Seen here is car No. 10 in 1906, one of two purchased from the Pacific Electric Railroad of Los Angeles and painted green. (SDHC.)

Bartlett sold SP&ES to SDERy on May 27, 1909, including all cars, three-and-a-half miles of track, and the car barn on Thirtieth Street, seen here with car No. 2 about 1906. Operation continued under the SP&ES name until 1915, when it was completely absorbed into the SDERy and all cars were repainted. The Broadway–Brooklyn Heights Line opened in 1909, using trackage from SP&ES. (SDHC.)

South Park was the first San Diego suburb to institute real estate covenants. Home prices were set to a minimum of $3,500 and no apartment buildings or liquor stores were permitted. Mission Hills enacted similar restrictive covenants in 1908 that also did not permit non-whites to purchase property. Seen here is SDERy car No. 2 at Twenty-Eighth and A Streets in 1906. This was one of the original double-decker cars, with the upper deck removed when remodeled in 1904. The

Broadway–Brooklyn Heights Line was extended to Thirtieth and Juniper Streets by June 1907, and free transfers to the SDERy system were offered to all South Park residents to keep total cost of travel to downtown to a nickel. Once the Switzer Canyon Bridge was completed in 1908, the line was extended to connect with the City Heights Line at University Avenue and Thirtieth Street. (SDHC.)

A new State Street Line from downtown was inaugurated in 1906 and extended to Old Town in 1910. That same year, Spreckels purchased the crumbling Estudillo adobe in Old Town and restored it as Ramona's Home, a tourist destination based on Helen Hunt Jackson's 1884 novel *Ramona*. New, larger California cars were added to the system in 1910 and 1911. Numbered 87 through 110, they were similar in design to the earlier cars but carried 44 passengers. Also in 1910, SDERy introduced a numbering system to replace route names. Seen here is car No. 103 serving Route 8 in Old Town in 1923, with Ramona's Home on the right. The building on the left was originally the home of Californio Juan Bandini. Over the years, it was variously the Cosmopolitan Hotel, a schoolhouse, an olive packing factory, and the Casa de Bandini restaurant. In 2012, it reopened as the Cosmopolitan Hotel and restaurant. (PSRM.)

A new Brill extended-length California car, No. 43, was added to the Coronado system in 1904. In 1906, SDERy car No. 11 was also added and renumbered car No. 44. Both can be seen here along with two trailer cars on the Orange Avenue Line around 1909. Also in 1906, electric service in Coronado was extended from the Hotel Del to Tent City. (CHA.)

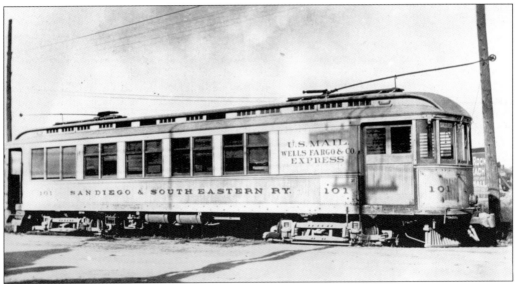

SDERy purchased the National City & Otay Railroad in 1906, converting a portion of it to interurban electric service to the south bay the following year as the San Diego Southern (later San Diego & Southeastern) Railway. Four coaches were transferred from the Coronado Railroad and renumbered 101 through 104. Car No. 101 is pictured around 1912, after it was reconfigured for combination passenger and express freight. (SDERA.)

Other interurbans were integrated into the SDERy system around this time. The Mexico & San Diego Railway (M&SD) connected Imperial Beach to National City and Otay beginning in 1910. The M&SD operated two battery-powered electric trolleys invented by Thomas Edison, hence the lack of wires in this 1910s photograph. Flooding during record-breaking rains in 1916 washed out the track, which was never repaired, ending the venture. (SDHC.)

The Point Loma Railroad (PLRR) was organized by real estate developer D.C. Collier. Rail was laid from just north of downtown for an eight-mile scenic loop through Loma Portal, Roseville, and Ocean Beach, beginning service in May 1909. After financial difficulties, Spreckels took over the line, absorbing it into the SDERy in 1922. PLRR car No. 109 is seen here in downtown San Diego in 1910. (SDERA.)

One of the main attractions on the PLRR route was Wonderland Park in Ocean Beach. Seen here on opening day on July 4, 1913, Wonderland was San Diego's first modern amusement park. It housed the first roller coaster on the West Coast, the Blue Streak Racer. Ten-cent admission also allowed access to a bowling alley, carousel, plunge pool, skating rink, and dance pavilion. (SDHC.)

Rides also included the Shoot-the-Chutes water slide, seen here in 1913. Billed as a wholesome family venue, a favorite Wonderland attraction was the animal menagerie, which included monkeys, bears, lions, leopards, and wolves, many of which later formed the basis for the San Diego Zoo. Attendance at Wonderland dropped after the opening of the Panama-California Exposition in 1915, and Wonderland closed its doors in 1916. (SDHC.)

The 1910s also saw the expansion of SDERy facilities. The powerhouse at Kettner Street and Broadway was upgraded. It is pictured here just after completion in 1911. A new car house and shops were opened on Fifteenth Street at Imperial Avenue the following year. In 1913, a car barn was constructed on Adams Avenue across from Mission Cliff Gardens. (SDERA.)

Car No. 107, pictured here around 1915 at the Imperial Avenue shops, was one of a series of 24 new cars numbered 87 through 110, built at the shops in 1910 and 1911. They were extended-length California cars with five center windows and long benches on each open end. The cars, which seated 44 passengers, were designed to accommodate increasing ridership due to the steady growth of San Diego. (SDERA.)

As ridership continued to increase, even more cars were needed to meet demand. With rapid advances in trolley car technology, SDERy discontinued its car building program. In 1912, a total of 24 cars were delivered from the St. Louis Car Company. These cars were numbered 125 through 148 and were collectively known as Class 1 cars. Seen here is car No. 125 on Broadway at Fifth Street around 1913. (SDHC.)

Class 1 cars were a new center-entrance design, called Pay as You Enter (PAYE), with the exit in the front near the driver. The cars were closed-body and seated 40 passengers. The interior of car No. 146 is seen here. Many older cars, including cars Nos. 1 through 8, were retired when the Class 1 cars arrived. (PSRM.)

The Panama-California Exposition opened in Balboa Park on January 1, 1915, celebrating the completion of the Panama Canal. Technological and cultural exhibits were housed in Spanish Baroque buildings designed by architect Bertram Goodhue. Other attractions included an Indian village, organ pavilion, and midway amusements. A trolley station was constructed on the east end of the exposition grounds running past a columned arcade, seen here in 1923. (PSRM.)

A popular method of traversing the extensive expo grounds was by electric-powered wicker carts. John D. Spreckels (right) and Joseph "Uncle Joe" Cannon, speaker of the US House of Representatives from 1903 to 1911, ride one of these "electriquettes" in 1915. In the background is the Home Economy Building on the Plaza de Panama. Many expo visitors returned to settle permanently in San Diego (SDHC.)

Needed for the increased traffic from 3.7 million visitors over the expo's two-year duration, 76 new cars were purchased, numbered 149 through 224. These were known as Class 2, or "Expo," cars. They served the Exposition Terminal on the Park Line, established in 1914, and throughout the SDERy network. Here, car No. 158 appears on State Street north of Market Street in 1914. (PSRM.)

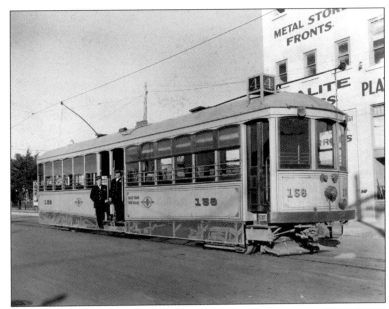

Class 2 cars were five feet longer than Class 1 cars and sat 52 passengers. A closed section in the rear was separated from the front by sliding doors. Interiors included electric lighting, window shades, and pull-cords to signal stops. Note the advertisements for Crisco shortening, Wrigley's gum, chiropractic care, and milk in car No. 190. (PSRM.)

The Class 2 cars were equipped for multiple-unit operation, allowing them to be connected in series and operated by a single motorman. Pictured is a Class 1 (left) and a Class 2 car on a rainy day on Ocean View Boulevard at Twenty-Eighth Street in the 1920s. (SDERA.)

After the expo, the tracks from the Balboa Park station were extended north along Park Boulevard to University Avenue. Crossing the canyons in between, three steel trestle bridges were constructed in 1917. Pictured here is car No. 221 on Bridge No. 3 in 1942. A new route, No. 7, ran from downtown, through the park, and across the trestles to terminate at Thirtieth Street and University Avenue. (PSRM.)

Five

UPGRADES AND APOGEE

Much of the SDERy track had been cobbled together from earlier rail lines during consolidation, and was not in very good condition. Even ties newly laid during the last decade could fare poorly underground. Upgrades were conducted across the SDERy system during the 1920s. Here, track workers stand with a collection of deteriorated wooden ties removed from Indiana Street north of Upas Street along Route 7 in 1924. (PSRM.)

Spreckels suffered financial difficulties after World War I, primarily related to wartime inflation and materials scarcity, as well as the high cost of completing the SD&A Railway through the mountains east of San Diego. The Golden Spike ceremony in the Carrizo Gorge is pictured here on November 15, 1919. Service began to Yuma after 12 years of construction. (PSRM.)

SDERy threatened to do away with the nickel trolley fare and cut service on some lines, but San Diego city officials successfully petitioned the California Railroad Commission to intercede. An agreement was reached that divided the city into inner and outer zones, with fares set at a nickel per zone. Here, new signage marks the zone boundary. (PSRM.)

Original redwood ties were pulled up and replaced with modern steel ties, as seen here on Twenty-Fifth Street at Broadway in 1924. Other sections received concrete ties. Sections of track on abandoned lines were pulled up and removed. A new line was added on Thirtieth Street between University and Adams Avenues in 1923, and the Market Street Line was extended to the cemeteries the following year. (PSRM.)

Once new rail was laid, the segments were welded together. After the street was repaved, track joints were ground to provide a smooth transition, as seen in this 1923 photograph taken on Fifth Street near Upas Street in what is today the Hillcrest neighborhood. Most system-wide track improvements were complete by the end of 1925. (PSRM.)

Upgrades to the original 1907 track on University Avenue just east of Park Boulevard are captured in this 1922 image. The arched concrete bridge, still in use today, replaced the original redwood one in 1914. In the background, the rapid growth of North Park can be seen. (Compare this to the photograph on page 66 from just 15 years earlier in 1907). (PSRM.)

Claus Spreckels had promised comfortable, modern trolley cars, and they began to arrive in late 1923. Fifty new cars were ordered, the finest available at the time, at a cost of $800,000. Designated Class 5, they were numbered 400 through 449. The cars were steel construction with closed bodies and had seats that could flip to face either direction. (PSRM.)

John D. Spreckels had long envisioned an electric interurban line to the beaches and up to La Jolla. This project began in 1923 with a viaduct over the Santa Fe Railroad tracks south of Old Town. Witherby Street was rerouted below the Santa Fe tracks, as seen here in 1924. Retired California cars were used to ferry workers and materials to the construction site. (PSRM.)

Here, two Class 5 cars can be seen on the completed viaduct in 1925. A temporary crossing was opened in 1924 to allow the line to continue to the beach communities. The Marine Corps Recruit Depot that had been built in 1919, where all Marine recruits west of the Mississippi River undergo basic training, appears in the background. (PSRM.)

Once across the viaduct, the SDERy line continued across the mud flats on the south side of Mission Bay, pictured here during construction around 1924. A branch line, Route 14, was run to Ocean Beach, where a new Egyptian-themed electrical substation was built. A four-day grand opening celebration of the new line began on May 1, 1924, with trolleys running every 20 minutes from Horton Plaza downtown. (SDERA.)

From the Ocean Beach branch line connection, the SDERy beach line followed the Bay Shore Railroad (BSRR) tracks, built in 1914 and taken over by Spreckels in 1923. BSRR car No. 82 is seen at Bacon and Voltaire Streets in 1923. The bridge across the mouth of Mission Bay was rebuilt, and the track was upgraded between the bridge and a new terminal at Mission Beach. (SDHC.)

A subway tunnel passed under the tracks from the Mission Beach terminal to reach the newly-constructed Mission Beach Amusement Center. The sign in this 1927 photograph reads, "Every SAT is play day at Mission Beach Amusements / Fun Devices, Surf and Plunge, Bathing / Dancing in Palatial Ballroom / Two free picnic pavilions." (SDHC.)

A popular attraction, still in operation today, is the Giant Dipper wooden roller coaster, seen here on opening day, July 4, 1925. To promote the new amusement park, a package deal was offered: for 75¢, patrons would receive a round-trip trolley ride from downtown, swimsuit use, a towel and locker, entrance to the swimming facilities, and lunch. The Mission Beach Amusement Center was renamed Belmont Park in 1955. (SDHC.)

From the Mission Beach Amusement Center, the beach line continued north to La Jolla. At Grand Avenue, the line ran on the abandoned Los Angeles & San Diego Beach Railroad grade. A new Mission Revival station was built at La Jolla Hermosa, near today's Bird Rock. Seen here in 1927, the station today houses the La Jolla United Methodist Church. (SDHC.)

The terminal station, surrounded by a turnaround loop, was built at Fay and Prospect Streets. The grand opening of the terminal was accompanied by the "Jollification," a celebration of the arrival of electric trolley service to La Jolla. Car No. 435 is seen here on the loop at the Fay Street terminal. (SDHC.)

The Class 5 cars were flexible: they could be individually operated, or several connected cars could be operated from the front car as multiple-unit trains. For the beach line, a three-car train would depart from downtown. After an 18-minute, six-mile run to the Ocean Beach junction, the rear car, serving Route 14, would decouple while in motion and turn off toward the station at Bacon and Voltaire Streets, as seen here in 1924. Two cars would continue north for another mile. There, the rear car, serving Route 15, would end at the Mission Beach Amusement Center. The final car, serving Route 16, would continue five more miles to La Jolla. Total travel time from downtown to La Jolla was only 35 minutes. Multiple-unit trains also served special events such as baseball games, as seen below on Kettner Street in 1948. (Above, SDHC; below, PSRM.)

SAN DIEGO ELECTRIC RAILWAY COMPANY

WEEKLY PASS

PRICE, $1.00

JANUARY 29 TO   FEB. 4, 1923 (Incl.)

Pass bearer on cars of the San Diego Electric Railway Company within the limits of the inner and outer zones for a period of seven (7) days as shown by the dates on the face of this pass.

Pass is to be shown Conductor or Operator at time of tendering fare and is good for only one (1) passenger on any given trip.

Not Valid

Unless Punched

W. P. 1
5651

GENERAL MANAGER

With the beach line completed, SDERy reached its maximum extent: the equivalent of 107 single-track miles. For comparison, Los Angeles's Pacific Electric Railway, the largest in the world in the 1920s, had approximately 1,000 miles of track. For context, compare San Diego's population growth from 1920 to 1930 of approximately 74,000 to 148,000 with Los Angeles's 575,000 to 1.24 million. System-wide single-fare weekly passes were introduced in 1923. (SDERA.)

Also in 1923, a new repair and paint shop was built at Fifteenth and K Streets to replace the original at Broadway and Kettner Street when that property was sold to San Diego Gas & Electric. Upgrades in Coronado included a new car house on First Street. A new loop track was installed at the ferry landing, seen here in 1924 with the ferries *Ramona* and *Morena* in the background. (PSRM.)

Six

DECLINE AND RESURGENCE

An influx of workers led to housing and transportation crises during the war years. New neighborhoods, such as Linda Vista, sprang up seemingly overnight, and zoning ordinances were changed to meet housing demand. Transportation needs were met by returning retired trolley cars to service, acquiring more from across the United States, and adding fleets of buses. Various trolleys and buses can be seen here at Horton Plaza in 1943. (SDHC.)

John D. Spreckels passed away on June 7, 1926. During four decades of development, he had seen San Diego grow from a bankrupt town of 16,000 to a bustling city of 135,000. Above, a horsecar travels on Fifth Street in 1887, the year Spreckels arrived. A similar view below shows the paved streets, electricity, and automobiles of San Diego around 1924. Claus Spreckels had been forced out of SDERy a year before his father's death. Liquidation of many Spreckels assets began when John D. Spreckels died, including the Mission Beach Amusement Center, the *San Diego Union* and *Evening Tribune* newspapers, the recently completed J.D. Spreckels Building on Broadway, and the San Diego & Arizona Railway. The SDERy, however, continued on under new management. (Above, PSRM; below, SDHC.)

Autobuses had already begun to intrude on trolley service in the 1920s, and expanded during the 1930s. The first trolley route to be completely replaced with bus service was Route 8, from downtown to Old Town, on May 1, 1924. The Route 8 SDERy bus appears here downtown at Horton Plaza on the first day of service. (PSRM.)

A portion of Route 4 from Thirty-Fourth Street to the cemeteries was replaced with buses later that year. Next to be replaced was the line over Point Loma between Roseville and Ocean Beach. Here, a bus drives on this route on Voltaire Street in 1925. Note the trolley wires still in place. (SDERA.)

Buses, like this stretch version in service at the 1935–1936 California Pacific International Exposition, were also used for special events. Held on the location of the 1915–1916 expo in Balboa Park, it was hoped the 1935–1936 expo would offset the economic downturn of the Great Depression. In the background of this image is the Maya-inspired Federal Building on Plaza de America. (PSRM.)

In the 1930s, a group of electric railway managers and streetcar manufacturers met to design a new streetcar that would counter passenger complaints and address bus incursion. The Presidents Conference Committee (PCC) car, introduced in 1935, was the result. SDERy purchased 28 PCC cars numbered 501 through 528, built by the St. Louis Car Company, in 1937 and 1938. Here is car No. 520 on Trias Street in Mission Hills. (SDHC.)

The PCC cars were greatly successful, with their quiet operation and excellent braking and acceleration. In San Diego, they were designated Class 6 cars and were first run on July 12, 1937, on Routes 1, 2, 3, and 7. SDERy's cars were painted in a cream-and-green color scheme adopted in 1931. Car No. 512 is pictured in the late 1930s at Thirtieth Street and Adams Avenue. (SDERA.)

Although they were financially profitable and well received by passengers, the PCC cars did not arrest the incursion of autobuses. PCC cars were a popular design across the United States, as well as Europe, with many still in operation today (see page 123). Pictured is a PCC car heading south on the Balboa Park trestle above Morley Field Drive and Florida Street in the 1940s. (PSRM.)

Two electric streetcars were purchased secondhand in 1938 from the Glendale & Montrose Railway in Los Angeles County, which ceased operations in 1930. Built in 1923 by American Car Company, these cars were numbered 351 and 352 and added to service on the Coronado Line, Route 20. Cars Nos. 147 and 352 are seen here in Coronado in 1946. (SDERA.)

Ridership declined throughout the Depression, resulting in the closure of several SDERy routes. Some were replaced with buses, including the National City interurban (1930), Ocean Beach (1938), and La Jolla (1940) lines. Others were discontinued, including La Playa (Route 13, in 1937) and Ocean View (Route 5, in 1938). Here, a Class 2 and a Birney car are seen on Broadway in the 1930s. (PSRM.)

By the end of the 1930s, only Routes 1 (Fifth Avenue), 2 (Broadway–Brooklyn Heights), 3 (Mission Hills), 4 (Imperial Avenue), 7 (East San Diego), 9 (Coronado Ferry), 11 (Adams Avenue), 12 (Logan Heights), and 20 (Orange Avenue) were still in operation. However, the advent of World War II led to an immediate need for increased public transportation. All Class 1, 2, and 3 cars that were available received a fresh coat of cream and green paint and were returned to service. Above, car No. 145 travels on a special "Parts Plant" route to the Consolidated Aircraft (later Convair) factory on Witherby Street in Middletown. Below is car No. 146 on Route 11. Note the advertisement for jobs for women at Convair. (Above, PSRM; below, SDERA.)

Additional cars were obtained from other electric trolley systems across the United States. Most of these were retired cars that were subsequently refurbished and returned to service in San Diego. The first to arrive were 16 cars from Salt Lake City's Utah Light and Traction Company. They were designated Class 8 and numbered 1001 through 1014. Car No. 1010 is seen here heading downtown. (SDERA.)

Next to arrive were 16 cars from Wilkes-Barre, Pennsylvania. Steel-bodied cars built in 1922, they were designated Class 7 and numbered 1015 through 1030. Car No. 1022 is pictured on Route 7 at University and Utah Street. These older cars were used to service the Parts Plant Routes 2, 7, 11, and 12. (SDERA.)

Twenty additional streetcars were received from New York's Third Avenue Railway System (TARS). These were dilapidated wooden cars built in 1905. They were quickly repaired and put into service, numbered 1031 through 1050 and designated Class 9. Here, car No. 1037 moves along Fifth Avenue and Broadway in 1946, with a PCC car in the background. (PSRM.)

The interior of car No. 1034 is seen here in 1947. Built by the Brill Company, these cars seated 44 passengers. More electrical power was needed to meet increased demand during wartime. New substations were built at the Adams Avenue car house, in the pedestrian subway of the Balboa Park station, and in the basement of the Spreckels Theater on Broadway. (SDERA.)

Here, car No. 1044 is on Broadway at India Street in 1946 serving Route 9, the Coronado Ferry Line. In the background is the Armed Services YMCA, built in 1924 in the Italian Renaissance style. The largest facility of its type in the United States, it served 25,000 servicemen daily, with hotel rooms, a gymnasium, an indoor pool, and various social activities. (PSRM.)

Six additional TARS cars were received in 1942. These were smaller than the original batch and were designed for subway use. These wooden cars built in 1907 and 1908 were numbered 1051 through 1056 and became Class 9 cars once in San Diego. Car No. 1055 serving Route 4 on Imperial Avenue is seen in this 1946 photograph. (PSRM.)

Streetcar ridership increased sixfold during the war. The V-J Day celebration appears here on August 14, 1945, on Broadway. Streetcars from Class 5, 8, and 9 are visible. After the war, Class 7 and 9 cars were kept on for Routes 3, 4, 9, and 12. Most of the remainder were retired. In the two years after the war, new track and routes were added to accommodate new residential areas and commute patterns, but ridership had dropped between 16 and 18 percent. A system-wide transit survey recommended ceasing operation on one-third of SDERy trackage. Regarding the 29 new diesel and gasoline buses ordered while the survey was being reviewed, SDERy assistant general manager R.F. McNally stated, "It is very expensive to dig up old track and replace it. . . . With buses, we do not have to go to that expense. Then, too, the buses are more flexible. In a city where population is growing and shifting as fast as it is in San Diego, we can shift our routes to meet changing needs faster than with street cars." (SDHC.)

Following the transit survey recommendation, Routes 1, 3, 4, 9, 12, and 20 were discontinued in 1946 and 1947. Route 1, the Fifth Avenue Line, ended service on June 30, 1946, coincident with construction of the Cabrillo Freeway bridge on University Avenue. It was replaced with bus service. Car No. 430 is pictured on Route 1 on University Avenue at Park Boulevard. (PSRM.)

The last run of Routes 4 (Imperial Avenue Line) and 12 (Logan Heights Line) took place on December 7, 1946. Fourteen new buses replaced the worn Class 7 TARS streetcars. Car No. 1034 is seen here serving Route 4 on Imperial Avenue around 1942. In the background, a billboard advertises $2.75 round-trip fares to Los Angeles on the Santa Fe Railroad. (SDERA.)

Route 20, the Orange Avenue Line in Coronado, saw its last day of service on May 31, 1947. Three days earlier, 39 new Convair "Liberator" buses had arrived to take over service throughout the SDERy system. After the war, Convair switched its production from bombers to buses. Here, car No. 1034 stops at the Coronado ferry slip in May 1947. (SDERA.)

The last run of Route 3 (Fifth Avenue–Mission Hills) took place on May 31, 1947. This line began with horsecar service on July 3, 1886. Route 20 (Orange Avenue) was also discontinued May 31, 1947. This removed the last of the Class 7 and 9 cars from service. Car No. 1031 is on Route 9 in Coronado in this 1940s photograph. (SDERA.)

From mid-1947 on, the only electric streetcar lines still in operation were the most heavily traveled: Routes 2 (Broadway–Brooklyn Heights), 7 (East San Diego), and 11 (Adams Avenue). Fifty Class 5 and 28 Class 6 (PCC) cars remained in service, complemented by 284 buses. On March 1, 1948, the SDERy, including all ferries and buses, was sold to J.L. Haugh and Western Transit Systems, an organization that ran bus and trolley systems in several Western states. On September 9, 1948, the company name was changed to San Diego Transit System. In January 1949, an application was made to the California Public Utilities Commission to discontinue all streetcar service and purchase 45 new buses. The application was approved on March 3, and the buses began to arrive that month. On April 23, 1949, the last day of streetcar service, a bus parade was held on Broadway, led by car No. 446, seen here. The banner on the trolley reads, "Retired with honor for a job well done." (PSRM.)

The late-night "owl" cars were the last to run on Routes 2, 7, and 11. On Route 11 (Adams Avenue), car No. 510 left Union Station (Santa Fe Depot) for its final run at 1:35 a.m. on April 24, 1949, driven by operator George Kimball. Car No. 408, Route 11, is pictured at Park Boulevard and Meade Avenue on March 23, 1948. (PSRM.)

Car No. 503, serving Route 2 (Broadway–Brooklyn Heights), left Union Station on its final run at 4:20 a.m. on April 24, 1949. Pictured is car No. 506 on its last day of operation on Route 2 along Thirtieth Street. It is led by car No. 505. In the background, a Class 5 car is visible. (PSRM.)

Cars Nos. 446 and 432, serving Route 7 (East San Diego), left Union Station at 4:25 a.m. on April 24, 1949, with operator J.N. Jacobs at the controls. Along with some commuting passengers were many VIPs, including J.L. Haugh, president of Western Transit Systems. Here, passengers are on the final run of car No. 446. (PSRM.)

Halfway through the final run, SDERy's most senior operator, N.A. Holmquist (with 42 years of service), took over the controls to the end of the line. The two cars then returned to the Adams Avenue car house, seen here, arriving at 5:35 a.m. San Diego became the first major city in the West to convert to all-bus operation. (PSRM.)

Seven

RETIREMENT AND RESTORATION

As old trolley cars were retired, many found new life as residences around San Diego. Several of the Class 2 cars that were retired in the 1930s were connected in pairs to form two-bedroom bungalows. Cars Nos. 170, 184, 156, 157, 155, and 151 are pictured at the corner of Laurel and India Streets in Bankers Hill about 1937. (PSRM.)

Some trolley cars were disposed of long before the end of SDERy. Seen here is a horse-drawn car converted into a shack. This 1959 photograph was taken at Thirty-Third and K Streets shortly before the car was collected by the Railway Historical Society of San Diego for restoration. (SDERA.)

Seen here in 1895 is a retired horse-drawn car converted to a playhouse for the Dodge family children. In front of the playhouse is Captain R.V. Dodge, his wife, Mary (left), and niece Julia. At far right is his son Richard Dodge, who later became a San Diego rail historian and author of *Rails of the Silver Gate: The Spreckels San Diego Empire.* (PSRM.)

Car No. 219 is pictured above on its final run from the Fifteenth Street and Imperial Avenue car house in April 1947. With the end of electric trolley service, the remainder of the Class 2 expo cars were dismantled and the car bodies moved to a storage yard in East San Diego. Below, from left to right, are cars Nos. 225, 222, 219, 218, and 221 at the storage yard. Prior to storage, the trucks and any other salvageable parts were removed, leaving only the wooden car bodies. The bodies were then advertised for sale for use as weekend cabins in the backcountry. Car No. 225 was bought and moved to 3218 Van Dyke Street, where it was converted into a small home (Both, PSRM.)

Many of the wooden Class 7 (Wilkes-Barre) and Class 9 (TARS) cars were moved to a storage yard at the foot of Fifteenth Street, not far from the car house. Above, several Class 9 cars are for sale, while below is a mix of Class 7 and Class 9 car bodies. However, the city council received several complaints about the Van Dyke Street expo car conversion, which violated zoning restrictions, and the council declared in May 1947 that no more streetcar bodies would be sold for reuse. The remaining cars were burned later that month. San Diego Transit was unable to find a buyer for the 50 Class 5 streetcars (number 400 through 449), and they were sold for scrap in 1952. (Both, PSRM.)

Many of the car bodies sold during the 1930s were turned into bungalow courts, like those shown here on Laurel Street in Bankers Hill. Other courts were constructed in Linda Vista and El Cajon. Although they were convenient during the housing shortage of the war years, most did not survive past the 1960s. (SDERA.)

Other trolley car bodies were relocated to San Diego's rugged backcountry and set up as vacation cabins, including several at Lake Morena. They were popular with families through the 1950s, but most of them were abandoned by the late 1960s. Here, car No. 187 sits near Lake Morena in 1971. An additional streetcar cabin is visible in the background at left. (SDERA.)

The trolley car bodies were a convenient size for a vacation cabin. The interior of car No. 201 is seen here in 1971, after more than two decades of use near Lake Morena. Built in 1914 for expo service by the St. Louis Car Company, car No. 201 was 48 feet and 7 inches long and originally seated 52 passengers. Many of the cars were outfitted with electricity and running water. Fittingly, Lake Morena is the result of another Spreckels-related project. Construction of the dam was begun in 1896 by the Southern California Mountain Water Company, formerly the Otay Water Company, one of J.D. Spreckels's first investments in San Diego. (Both, SDERA.)

Other cars were converted for use as offices or commercial space. On February 1, 1947, car No. 150 was relocated to 2154 Logan Avenue in Barrio Logan, above. Car No. 150 was a Class 2 streetcar built by McGuire in 1914. It was in service through 1940, when it was retired, but was brought back into service during the war. After its second retirement in 1947, it was enclosed by stucco walls, below, and opened as a diner. As the neighborhood demographics changed over the years, so did the restaurant. Until recently, the trolley was home to a Mexican restaurant, El Nuevo Carrito. It is currently closed, but expected to reopen soon serving Cuban fare. (Both, PSRM.)

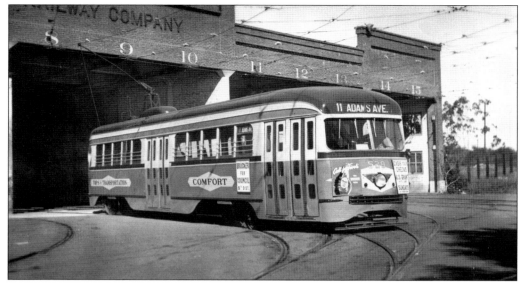

Two PCC cars were sold to the Orange Empire Railway Museum in Parris, California, including car No. 528, seen here leaving the Adams Avenue car house in the 1940s. Another six PCC cars were sold for scrap in 1957. Seventeen PCC cars were sold to the El Paso City Lines in Texas in 1950, and three more followed in 1952. (PSRM.)

The 20 PCC cars were used on El Paso's International Line serving Juarez, Mexico, as the only electric streetcar line to cross an international border. Unlike many electric trolley routes in the 1950s, El Paso's International Line flourished. San Diego's PCC cars served El Paso until they were retired in 1974. Seen here is car No. 509, one of the cars sold to El Paso, at the Balboa Park station in 1947. (SDERA.)

Facilities were also disposed of. Some, like the former SDERy streetcar repair shop at Fifteenth Street and Imperial Avenue, pictured here in 1972, were modified to accommodate buses. Upgraded over the years, the entire block now houses the maintenance, repair, and storage facilities for the Metropolitan Transit System's bus fleet. (SDERA.)

The former car barn on Adams Avenue, seen here in 1974, was bought by the San Diego Paper Box Company and used for manufacturing. The building was torn down in 1979 to make room for condominiums. Mission Cliff Gardens across the street, which had been closed in 1930, was reopened in 1991 as Trolley Barn Park; today, it hosts picnickers and a free summer concert series. (PSRM.)

For over 30 years, San Diego public transportation consisted solely of buses. However, in 1979, Metropolitan Transit System (taken over by the city of San Diego in 1967) purchased the abandoned San Diego & Arizona Eastern right-of-way and spent the next two years converting it to electric light rail service, the first of the "second generation" trolley systems in the United States. Pictured is the grand opening run on July 26, 1981, on C Street. (SDHC.)

The first Metropolitan Transit System (MTS) trolley cars were the U2 model built by Siemens-Düwag of Germany, originally designed for the Frankfurt U-Bahn. The last of them were retired in 2015. Now considered historic trolleys themselves, one is in active service at the heritage railroad at the Orange Empire Rail Museum in Parris, California, seen here in early 2017. (OERM/AD.)

Car No. 54 has a long history in San Diego. It was constructed at the SDERy car shops in 1902, using parts from two cars from the Citizens Traction Company (see page 60). After it was retired in 1914, the body of car No. 54 was used as an office, guest apartment, and storage in various east San Diego locations, as seen here around 1957. (SDERA.)

After being acquired by the Railway Historical Society of San Diego, car No. 54 was restored and displayed at the Whaley House in Old Town and then the San Diego Historical Society in Balboa Park. It is now on display at the San Diego Electric Railway Association in National City, where it awaits further restoration under a new car barn, pictured here. (AD.)

Other San Diego streetcars are undergoing restoration as well. PCC car No. 508 was acquired by the Orange Empire Rail Museum in Parris, California, in 1957. After years of outdoor display, car No. 508 is currently indoors and undergoing the final touches of restoration. Once complete, it will be in active service on the museum's vintage railway. (OERM/AD.)

Car No. 1043 was one of the few TARS cars not destroyed after the war. Purchased by the Bay Area Electric Railway Association in 1947, it became part of the Western Railway Museum in Suisun City, California, in 1964. It can be seen here in a storage yard in Oakland, California, in 1948, next to a Birney car, formerly SDERy car No. 301. (PSRM.)

Nostalgia for the old trolley cars is not limited to rail buffs. Communities across San Diego use the trolleys to construct their neighborhood identities. University Heights, home to Mission Cliff Gardens and the Adams Avenue car barn, incorporated the trolley into the neighborhood sign on Park Boulevard. Ostriches, reminiscent of those once housed at Mission Cliff Gardens, top the streetlights that support the sign. (DM.)

In South Park, the Station Tavern occupies the lot where the South Park & East Side Railroad and later SDERy tracks cut diagonally between Thirtieth Street and Fern Street. The restaurant décor is trolley themed, including a miniature replica streetcar in the children's playground along the former right-of-way. (DM.)

San Diego's Metropolitan Transit System (MTS) is capitalizing on the public's nostalgia for the historical streetcars. Beginning in 2005, MTS acquired several PCC cars originally built between 1946 and 1948 and used in San Francisco, St. Louis, and Philadelphia. The cars were restored in partnership with the San Diego Electric Railway Association and given the historical cream-and-sage paint scheme. In 2011, car No. 529 inaugurated the Silver Line, a downtown loop approximating the former Ferry Line. Pictured is car No. 529 on the Silver Line in 2016. Restored PCC car No. 530 has also begun service, with more on the way. Another organization, San Diego Historic Streetcars, is in the process of restoring SDERy car No. 138, a Class 1 car built in 1912. The goal is to return car No. 138 to service once restoration is complete. (Both, AD.)

After the last run of the trolleys in 1949, San Diego Transit System was given two years to remove wires and tracks. Wire removal began on May 23, 1949, with the Union Station (Santa Fe Depot) loop. Many tracks, especially those laid on concrete ties, were left in place and paved over with asphalt. Pictured is exposed 1914 rail on University Avenue near the Georgia Street Bridge during utility work in 2015. (AF.)

However, the SDERy system is resurfacing, literally. The buried tracks pose a hazard to construction. Consequently, most rail is pulled up and discarded when encountered. The rail seen here was removed from Twenty-Eighth Street during a construction project in 2015 and donated to the San Diego Electric Railway Association for display at its museum in National City. (AF.)

When historical resources are expected to be found during a construction project, city guidelines require archaeologists to be on hand to record any discoveries. While historical documents may mark the location of previous trolley tracks, unexpected discoveries like the brick-lined track segment found here on University Avenue in North Park in 2015 can provide information never written down. (DM.)

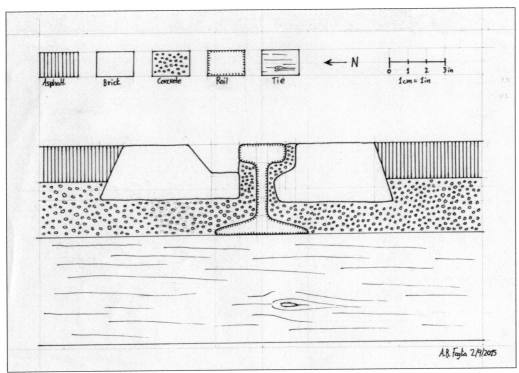

Archaeology is, by its nature, a destructive process. Extensive documentation is essential, since there is only one opportunity to excavate an archaeological site. Seen here is a field sketch of the brick-lined rail shown in the top photograph, drawn by archaeologist Alberto Foglia in 2015. Technical illustrations like this are useful to future researchers who are unable to view the historic material firsthand. (AF.)

Because most trolley tracks are under existing roads, there is still a lot of rail likely to be uncovered. The city and San Diego Gas & Electric have a long-term ongoing plan to move all electric, cable, and telecom utilities underground, neighborhood by neighborhood. Here, tracks uncovered in 2015 along Twenty-Eighth Street at A Street in Golden Hill can be seen. (AF.)

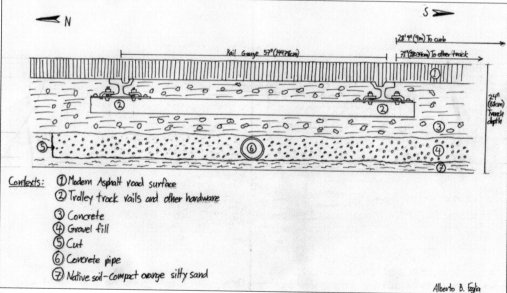

Pictured here is a subsurface profile sketch by archaeologist Alberto Foglia of the track and associated roadbed on Twenty-Eighth Street shown in the top photograph. By combining historical documents with material remains still present underground, there is much that can still be learned about the early trolley systems of San Diego. (AF.)

BIBLIOGRAPHY

Amero, Richard W. *Balboa Park and the 1915 Exposition*. Charleston, SC: The History Press, 2013.

Bugbee, Susan H. *South Park: San Diego, California*. San Diego, CA: self-published, 2010.

Copeland, Allen P. "San Diego and the PCC Streetcar." Metropolitan Transit System, 2012. www.sdmts.com/sites/default/files/attachments/san_diego_pcc_pallen.pdf

Covington, Donald B. *North Park: A San Diego Urban Village, 1896–1946*. San Diego, CA: Hon Consulting, Inc., for the North Park Community Association History Committee, 2007.

Crawford, Richard W. *San Diego Yesterday*. Charleston, SC: The History Press, 2013.

Dodge, Richard V. *Rails of the Silver Gate: The Spreckels San Diego Empire*. San Marino, CA: Golden West Books, 1960.

———. "Primal Electric Transit in San Diego." *Dispatcher*, issue 34: November 15, 1960. Railway Historical Society of San Diego.

Engstrand, Iris H.W. *San Diego: California's Cornerstone*. Tulsa, OK: Continental Heritage Press, 1980.

Enneking, William C. "Those Fabulous Cable Cars." *Journal of San Diego History, Volume 2, Number 1*: January 1956. San Diego Historical Society.

Freeberg, Ernest. *The Age of Edison: Electric Light and the Invention of Modern America*. New York, NY: The Penguin Press, 2013.

Jackson, Kenneth T. *Crabgrass Frontier: The Suburbanization of the United States*. New York, NY: Oxford University Press, 1985.

Mengers, Douglas Wayne. "Tracks and Tracts in America's Finest City: An Historical Archaeology of San Diego's Early Trolley Suburbs." Master's thesis, San Diego State University, 2016.

Pourade, Richard F. *The History of San Diego, Volume Four: The Glory Years*. San Diego, CA: The Union-Tribune Publishing Company, 1964.

Sanders, Eric. "The Story of Car 54." *The Trolley Lines*. San Diego Electric Railway Association, June 2012.

University Heights Historical Society. *Cable Cars and Ostrich Feathers: A Self-Guided Walking Tour of Historic University Heights*. San Diego, CA: Save Our Heritage Organization, 2006.

About the San Diego Electric Railway Association

The San Diego Electric Railway Association (SDERA) is dedicated to the preservation of the history of the San Diego Electric Railway, San Diego's primary streetcar system, which operated from the late 1800s to 1949. The San Diego Electric Railway Association exists to:

- Preserve the artifacts and equipment of the San Diego Electric Railway and other related local companies.
- Establish and maintain an active railway museum, complete with an operating, historic streetcar line.
- Serve as an educational resource showing the important roles streetcars, interurbans, and electric railways played in the development of the San Diego area.
- Preserve past and present pictures, publications, and artifacts of the current San Diego Trolley.

SDERA is also the operator of the National City Depot, a historic Santa Fe railroad station. The association operates a railroad and local history museum within the depot, and the depot is open Saturday and Sunday from 10:00 a.m. to 4:00 p.m. A large model-railroad exhibit, operated by our 3-Rail model railroad group, is also included in the museum displays. All train buffs, local historians, and people looking for an interesting day out in the San Diego area are encouraged to visit the depot, join the association, and help the depot grow into a major destination within San Diego County. Financial and equipment gifts from people, corporations, and organizations interested in preserving San Diego's railway history make SDERA's work possible.

General meetings are typically held at the National City Depot every three months: February, May, August, and November on the second Saturday night of the month at 6:15 p.m. There is no charge to attend these meetings, which cover interesting subjects relating to past, present, and future electric railways. Plan to arrive by 6:00 p.m. to chat and peruse the gift shop.

San Diego Electric Railway Association
National City Depot
922 W. Twenty-Third Street
National City, CA 91950
619-474-4400
www.sdera.org

DISCOVER THOUSANDS OF LOCAL HISTORY BOOKS
FEATURING MILLIONS OF VINTAGE IMAGES

Arcadia Publishing, the leading local history publisher in the United States, is committed to making history accessible and meaningful through publishing books that celebrate and preserve the heritage of America's people and places.

Find more books like this at
www.arcadiapublishing.com

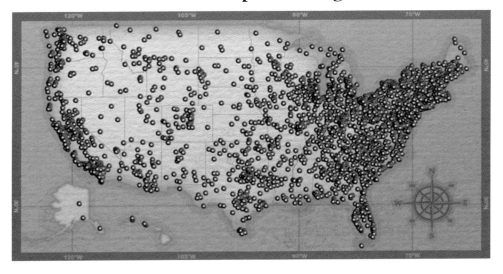

Search for your hometown history, your old stomping grounds, and even your favorite sports team.